MIDDLE-CLASS SIDEWINDER

BY – DOROTHY BROWN PERKINS

Contact: Dorothy Brown Perkins
Email: dbperkins@hotmail.com

RCS Publishing, Leah G. Reynolds
Rcspublishingandmediagrp.com

What is your legacy? Join Dorothy Brown Perkins as she shares a story about her life, heritage, and gifted children. This story's setting is within a small western town in Michigan where Billy grew up with his dad, mother, brother, and sister. Billy is the oldest son in the family. He is Black, curious, gifted, and a mischievous child in the story. On the outside, he is sweet, charming, full of old loving grace, loved by his parents, admired by everyone. But, Billy's mother had an uneasy feeling about him.

Wise well beyond his years, Billy has always been a free spirit or, in other terms, a "Sidewinder." His brilliance led him to attend one of the most prestigious academies in Indiana. When the school Masters took him on their senior class trip to Europe for two weeks. Billy left the group and decided to be like an adult.

Acknowledgments

I would like to acknowledge my daughter, Sandy Elizabeth Perkins Hollie, a friend, Jackie Jones and my son-in-law, Curtis Hollie, Jr., who reviewed the early drafts of the manuscript and finally, my sons, Billy Perkins, Randy Perkins, daughter-in-law, Jocelyn Perkins who offered their comments through the writing process and "My Grands" Amya Perkins, Elizabeth Perkins, William Perkins, Joshua Hollie, and Justin Hollie who offered me love and patience.

"Your legacy is every life you touch" – Maya Angelou

Table of Contents

Introduction

What does a legacy mean to you? When I reflect upon my life, I am reminded that a legacy is not what we leave tomorrow when we are gone, but what we have given, created, impacted while here that will continue to live. My name is Dorothy Perkins. I am a mother of three, a grandmother of five, and a dedicated Educator.

My story began 75 years ago in Cotton Plant, a small Arkansas town located 60 miles outside of Memphis, TN. I was raised on a farm with my four siblings. My parents raised four children to adulthood; before my three siblings, and I were born. Having older siblings made life more enriching as a young child.

My nieces and nephews were the same age as I. When school dismissed for the summer, I would travel on the train from Arkansas to Chicago, St. Louis, and California to babysit for my siblings. I was eleven years old and a solo traveler. I enjoyed traveling because I could meet and talk to new people.

My eldest sister lived around the corner from the train station in Chicago. She would meet me at the station, and we would walk home together and talk about my trip. My family traveled often to visit my other siblings. We traveled from our home in Northern Arkansas to Memphis, St. Louis, and Chicago.

Seeing the U.S. via car and train were beautiful sights to witness. It stoked a love for traveling that I still carry in my heart.

Education was also at the forefront of our lives. Although we were raised on a farm, both of my parents ensured that we attended school every day. While some of my classmates were forced to work on their family farms during the seasons, my father declared that all of his children would receive an education.

Both my mother and grandmother were educators. I watched the joy on their faces when they spoke about their day working with students. I performed well in high school and was accepted into the University without delay.

I decided to pursue a career in education at the University of Arkansas. I financed my education by working at several factories in Chicago. My jobs paid for tuition as well as room and board at school. We were blessed to have had the summer opportunities to work. Cotton Plant was home to factories and farming. At one point, over one million acres of land was cultivated for cotton alone.

Kellogg's home was in Cotton Plant as well as Tyson Food, Butterball, and many more. Most of the town residents were either farmers or employed at the factories.

After graduation from high school, I began working an internship in Michigan with another teacher, and we became fast friends. The internship was offered to honor students, and it lasted for the entire summer semester. She was doing her internship with a sixth-grade teacher, and we shared notes about our experiences in school and practicum.

The practicum included teaching fellow educators and peers. I remember several of the professors from the University vividly. They wore suits and dresses daily.

Women wore heels and carried their books and walking shoes in an attaché case. They were so sophisticated and cosmopolitan.

After the internship concluded, I began working for the Albion Public School System. There were only a few Black teachers in the area, so we all got together often to unwind. It was a wonderful environment for us, and we kept each other supported.

I met a fellow educator from the nearby private boys' school named Arthel Wyre. We became close friends and would often hang out together with the other educators in the area. Arthel's wife taught within the Albion Public Schools as well.

One day Arthel approached me and excitedly announced that his cousin was heading into town from Los Angeles for a visit. I didn't think much of his statement until he playfully added, "I told him all about you, and I really want you to meet him." His cousin arrived in Michigan on a Friday after our classes commenced.

After work, we gathered at a farmhouse located in Albion, where everyone would listen to music, dance, eat, and just hang out. We were all young teachers and enjoyed the safe and comfortable place to unwind. The farmhouse was a nicely decorated well laid out building.

I was seated on the couch listening to music when Mac approached me. I was taken aback by how kind and handsome he was. We immediately hit it off and began courting. He and I fell in love. Based on the time that we shared with each other and the fun we had together, we knew that our love was destined to last.

We met in April 1969 and were engaged by May of that same year. We were married on August 2, 1969. We settled in Albion, Michigan, and purchased our first home together. Our union was blessed with three children Billy, Randy, and Sandy.

This is where our legacy began.

1 Corinthians 13:13

And now abide faith, hope, love, these three; but the greatest of these is love.

Chapter 1 – Family

Watching my children grow from birth to adulthood has been one of my greatest blessings. My children have surprised me in ways that I couldn't imagine. Their intellect and compassion were unmatched even as young children.

I noticed just how gifted my children were when my eldest son Billy was born, and I was able to observe his intelligence in action. Billy came into this world on March 23, 1971. Our lives changed forever after that wonderful moment.

Growing up, my parents instilled within us a supreme desire for education. I made sure that my children were prepared for school and supported throughout. My children thanked me by expanding my world and my knowledge about life's possibilities.

This story is about my son Billy. He is my Middle- Class Sidewinder. An intelligent, independent thinker Billy stood out as the person who was driven by self more so than outside forces.

From the moment he entered this world, I knew that he was unique. Billy has always had a zest for knowledge and a passion for living his life to the fullest. He started talking in complete sentences when he was just 10 months old. Ms. Moss, Billy's baby-sitter, was a retired schoolteacher and took note of the special gift that Billy had. Ms. Moss was a remarkable woman. She was eighty years old, still driving a car, I know amazing, right? She was truly a Christian, nurturing, loving, and caring woman sent from God to take care of our precious little bundle of joy.

She took Billy on a short field trip in his all- weather stroller every day when the weather was permissible. You know how the weather can be in Michigan, sometimes unpredictable. There was a long trail within our neighborhood, where Ms. Moss would walk with

Billy. While on her adventures, she talked about everything they saw and observed all things about nature. My son absorbed this information like a sponge. As Billy was riding in his stroller down the path, he listened and engaged in the conversation with her.

She remarked about how he babbled happily while she talked about the vegetation, squirrels, and trees.

Even though he was young, she still knew he understood the conversation. A few months before he was a year old, he started a real conversation with me. Billy was unusually alert even as an infant. His deep penetrating eyes seemed to scan a room observing everything around him.

I know it sounds odd, but Billy's quick wit and intelligence were alarming at first. As a first time parent, raising children was a bit intimidating. I was prepared to educate and support my children but not for answering some of the questions that Billy asked at such a young age. He seemed to be a deep well of intrigue, taking in his surroundings and questioning everything around him like a scholar.

The minute he became a big brother, I witnessed his tender-heartedness and attentiveness. He immediately became my little helper.

Randy was born on July 7, 1972. Randy is my second child, and he is Billy's only brother. It was a very hot day in July, and Billy said to me, "Mommy, I love our baby, and I want to hold him on my lap. Please, let me help you take care of our baby because he is so little, he cannot talk, walk, and he doesn't have teeth to eat." From that moment of those very words, I knew Billy was something special.

He helped with the baby by getting items such as diapers, lotion, comb, brush, Q-tips, and throwing away dirty diapers, and any other small things that I needed for Randy. Billy was so proud of doing his jobs for our new baby.

Growing up, they were very close and did everything together, just like twins. If you saw one of them, then you saw the other. Always his protector, Billy became attentive to his needs and made sure to vocalize them to me.

Billy had an obsession with milk as a toddler, and he would, on several occasions, drink all of his milk and his brother's as well. Often he would come running to tell me that "the baby's milk is all gone, mommy" and that I needed to fix him some more, not revealing to me that he was the culprit behind the finished milk. Even at that age, he was very clever.

Growing up, Billy loved to watch television and was so fascinated by what he saw; he often discussed what he watched on television with me. As he was watching a Western one day, he asked me why the man who was riding the horse was called a cowboy and instead of a horsee-boy? "That animal is a horse and not a cow." I was flabbergasted! He was only fifteen months old when he discovered this. I said, "you're right, Billy, that is a horse and not a cow." He would scrutinize all situations in that manner.

Billy recognized most of the letters and sounds at two years old, making him ready for a private preschool. He enjoyed reading books and was a very fluent reader at the age of three years old. He was very busy and curious about everything. Even though Billy was fifteen and a half months older than Randy, they were still very close.

He was also very determined. Everything that Billy attempted to do he succeeded. Some things he skipped right over. He taught himself to ride his bike at two years old, so there was never a need for training wheels. When he didn't understand something, he asked questions without hesitation. Everything was Black or White with Billy. There was very little room for grey areas with my son.

I was blessed to have a lovingly close family. Our children cared about each other, and they were also protective of one another. It warmed our hearts to see the love between my children. My husband, Mac, worked as a Transportation Engineer in Detroit, so I was home with the children most of the time. I enjoyed spending time with them because they were so much fun. They could make up their own games to play and would entertain themselves. They all loved reading and could sit with their books in their little laps, getting lost in their stories.

All three of the children loved when their father returned home from work. He spent quality time with each one of them. They all looked up to Mac, but my husband was Billy's superhero. Mac was away from the home quite a bit because his job was very demanding. Mac was a devoted father, loving husband, and loyal community member. He was a trustee in the church, he drove the church van and also taught Sunday school.

The boys had a loving relationship with their father. Mac would always take them to the barbershop every other Saturday morning.

Growing up, Billy loved playing basketball in the backyard with his dad. That is one of the many hobbies and memories they shared together.

We raised our children in a very small town called Heaven, Michigan, which was about one hundred miles west of Detroit. There were many small farms nearby with mostly cows, chickens, goats, sheep, and pigs. It was approximately fourteen thousand people in our town. It was a great town to raise a family.

Our little town was a nice one. Oh, how we welcomed everyone to our community despite what background they came from; it was very diverse.

Everybody knew each other, so it was a very safe place to be. We all attended many gatherings in our schools, churches, and libraries. On the weekends, we took the children downtown and walked along the sidewalk while enjoying popcorn or ice cream. We frequently visited the movie theatre and purchased items for the kids from nearby shops. Those were great memorable times.

The kids of Heaven were highly educated. Most of them left home and went to universities, colleges, armed forces, trade schools, and blue-collar jobs. We have an excellent college in our community, which attracted people from all over the world to attend. Parents and teachers had an excellent rapport with the community, and we were proud.

Chapter 2 - Early Childhood

As Billy grew from infancy into early childhood, I witnessed his unique take on things around him. He was a happy child, but he was also quite shy and cautious. I had to be careful of what I said to him because he took everything literally.

Billy and Randy went off to school after their preschool programs. They headed to their elementary school located in the neighborhood; most days, they dressed alike, looking like twins. They were each other's best friend and wanted to be in the same activities.

On Billy's first day of school, his dad took him. He kissed him goodbye for the day. As his father turned to leave, Billy yelled, "I don't think I want to go to school this year! So, take me to the Child Care Center. I promise you; I'll come back for Kindergarten next year." His father watched curiously as Billy tried to reason his way out of school. "This place is too BIG, and I am too LITTLE to be here all day with these STRANGERS," he explained.

Billy continued to say, "You told me not to talk to strangers. I cannot sit here all day and not talk to these strangers. It will be boring." His dad explained to him that he is five years old and he must start school this year.

Billy listened intently as his father spoke while processing the entire situation. Mac was tickled by the way his son thought. At times Billy reasoned like an adult. Mac kneeled down to meet his son at eye level and spoke softly.

"The other boys and girls in the classroom are five years old, too. They are new to the school, also. So, no one is a stranger." After his dad told him that Billy agreed to stay at his new school.

One day after Kindergarten classes ended, Billy came home excited to share what he learned. I listened intently as he clarified, "Ooh Mama, we have been calling this word the wrong thing. You know when you urinate in the bathroom? We've been saying the wrong word, it's pee!" he announced. I stifled my laughter and told him that the proper word was urinate.

He kept us on our toes.

During a parent/teacher conference, his teacher pulled me aside and informed me that I had a gifted child on my hands. I smiled knowingly at my precocious little boy. I took Randy and Billy to the Library weekly. Billy managed to check out stacks of books each time. By the end of each week, Billy had completed every book that he borrowed.

One evening after my husband and I tucked the boys in to sleep, Randy came running into our room. "Billy is reading, and it's keeping me awake," he announced sleepily. I wondered how Billy could still be reading when we turned the lights out. I walked into their room to find Billy holding his father's large flashlight under the covers. There was never a dull moment with my children.

Billy was the greatest achiever in the Kindergarten class. His work was done first and always, perfect. He loved his teacher and all the boys and girls. He helped others who needed assistance. He was very talkative and active. All the children liked him. He was a proficient reader. Billy had a powerful vocabulary. He used big words.

During a parent teacher conference, his teacher said, "He is fun and humorous all the time." She was 100% correct. Billy told stories that kept us laughing. I don't think he realized just how funny he was, however. I think in his mind, he was simply telling the story how he saw it. Dinner was a time for our family to share stories and connect.

Billy spoke about the school day every night at dinner. Billy went into a detailed story about his day. "Ghee, Jane had a big water puddle around her chair. I don't know why she didn't go to the restroom. She did not get up. She is so afraid of being in the classroom until she urinated her pants. She never gets out of her chair.

She just stays and never gets-up for anything. I know she's too tired when she leaves school." He relayed this story with an amusingly astonished look on his face. He didn't question why Jane wet her pants; his young mind had rationalized Jane's behavior all on his own.

One day, the teacher gave Billy a new job to do! His job was to help a student named Jack in the classroom to identify each letter of the alphabet. Billy said, "I keep showing and telling him the names of the letters. He gets so confused sometimes and does not know the letters from the numbers. I hope he'll remember the names of all the letters. I'm trying so hard to help him identify the letters. I don't understand why he cannot remember the letters. Those letters are easy to remember."

Billy thought that his class and teacher were the best in the whole wide world. He felt responsible for helping his classmates. When Billy got back home from school, he said, "Mrs. Suesack will be leaving the class for the second part of the year to have her baby. Another teacher will take her place."

When Billy heard this news, he said, "I am wondering if the teacher is her mother. If she is her mother, we will still have the best class in the whole wide world." I was proud to see that my shy, young boy concerned himself so much about his teacher's wellbeing and the behavior of his class.

He came home from school and announced, "Our teacher's last day was today. I feel all mixed-up for school tomorrow." I sent him off to school the next day and watched as he climbed the steps on the bus. I knew that the substitute had better be on her 'A' game whomever she was because Billy expected his class to continue as it had with Mrs. Suesack at the helm.

To my surprise, he arrived home with a look of sadness on his face. When I asked him what was wrong, he threw his hands up and said, "Our new teacher came to our class today. Mother, you will have to come to school with me tomorrow! Our new teacher is mixed-up. She doesn't do like Mrs. Suesack. The kids are all up and running around in the room. I need to call Mrs. Suesack and tell her the bad news about the children. Do you have her number? So, I can tell her to get us another teacher."

I told him that, "this wasn't true that all teachers are good teachers. They just all have different styles of teaching. It will get better. I once worked with your new teacher, and I know her personally. She is a very good teacher, so everything will be fine. "

He didn't seem too convinced by my words. Billy simply responded, "I hope so." The rest of the year was just great for him. Billy moved on to the first grade, and he and his teacher had an excellent rapport. He stayed ahead of his class and received several awards for those years. He was voted the most outstanding student for first and second grades.

Billy and Randy both excelled in school. Their years in grade school were enlightening and enriching. If you had heard them talk about their school, you would have thought they entered an Ivy League University. They spoke so highly about their teachers and what they learned. One thing I admired about the school was it was very clean, and everyone was well respected.

While attending school, the children had a dress code, such as wearing regular shoes. They carried their tennis shoes in their gym bags for physical education during the school day. In the winter, boots were pulled off at the door, and shoes were put on. Every morning, the old white-haired principal greeted the children at the door.

Even though she was a quiet lady, everyone still listened to what she had to say and followed her instructions.

All the teachers greeted the boys and girls at their doors with a friendly, "Good Morning," calling the children by their names. Teachers did an excellent job of communicating with the parents concerning the student's involvement in class using monthly letters, homework, phone calls, parent meetings, room-parents and information was sent home frequently.

The parents did a very good job of supporting their children's academics, and like the old saying goes, "It takes a village to raise a child." The whole community got involved, also the private college.

Around this time, we were blessed with another addition to the family. On May 13, 1978, my only daughter, Sandy, was born. Billy was eight years old when his sister was born, and he was so excited. Sandy was Billy's Queen Elizabeth, and he was very protective of her, and he treated her like royalty.

Nobody was allowed to touch her or harm her in any way, and Billy made sure of this. Growing up, Sandy loved hanging out with her friends from church and school and insisted them to come home with her to play dolls and watch movies.

Chapter 3 - Third Through Eighth Grades

Billy took The College Board, Scholastic Aptitude Test, and the SAT in middle school, which he scored at a high school level. He was placed in the "Gifted Program." He competed with students from all over the county. He was an avid reader.

Billy was a wellspring of knowledge, and reading was his preferred way of learning. If we went shopping, we knew where to find him. We could find him in the books store sitting on the floor reading.

Third grade is a transitional year from lower elementary to upper elementary. There are many changes associated with school progression. Various new places, things, activities, and course topics are added to the curriculum as students move up. This is also a year when some students struggle with the transition.

Billy was extremely interested in Science, Math, and Reading. He learned very easily and was much self-directed. He asked many in-depth questions during a lesson and used research methods to help find the answers. He was extremely curious and possessed a well-developed sense of humor.

Growing up, he needed extra stimulation that would give him a greater challenge. He completed learning center activities almost as soon as they became available. He was an overachiever and an outstanding student. Billy was placed in the Gifted program, which he remained throughout middle school.

Billy was involved in extracurricular activities growing up in school, such as Cub Scouts. I was the Den Leader for approximately twenty-eight boys at his school. We met once a week. They had many activities. One was to make a racing car out of a block of wood and shape it and design a car of their choice.

The racecar had to be a certain weight in order to be qualified to race, and the parents would help their kids make and design these cars. They would race the car on three different race tracks, and all the boys would have a chance to race their car, and it was a first, second, third place winner. Billy's dad and I helped them build the racecars.

Billy and Randy had piano lessons once a week. They practiced at home every day. I waited in the car until they got done with their lessons. The kids at school started teasing Billy; so he asked me could he please stop the lessons since he had so many more activities to do. I gave in to him.

Every second Sunday at our church was Youth Sunday, and all the music students were given the opportunity to perform one of their songs they had learned to play in their piano classes. All the kids were praised for showing their talents to the church community. Randy continued to play piano until he was in high school.

Another activity Billy and Randy played was flag football with the City's Recreation Department. There were many boys involved in the programs, which allowed for several teams in the division. We competed among ourselves. It was great fun watching the competition between the boys and the other competitors.

During the 4th -8th grade Billy and Randy were in the basketball league for their conference. Billy was very good at basketball and was known for his famous three-point shots. The boys always showed excellent sportsmanship when playing the game.

Randy was on the Cross Country team for the local high school. I helped out with the Cross Country team as one of the assistant leaders with the girls' team. Randy would have practice every day on the weekday. During the season, he practiced and trained running every day. He was so dedicated and determined. Once during the season on a Saturday, we went to the Sand Dunes in Indiana. There they had a special practice.

We had so much fun!

My husband and I would not allow the boys to spend the night outside of our home for safety reasons. Instead, we hosted large sleepovers where over 15 boys would stay with us for the evening. The kids would laugh and play all night. In the morning, I made them bacon, eggs, and pancakes which they devoured happily.

We had one kid who moved to Lansing, Michigan, which was over an hour away, but he always visited our home for sleepovers with the other children. It was wonderful. At the time, we owned an Apple computer, which the children took turns playing games. The kids grew quite proficient with the computer.

In the summer, we took our kids on extended road trips. We started in Michigan and would drive to Washington, DC, then to Louisiana and all the way to Los Angeles to visit family along the way. We visited my parents and my husband's family, as well. It was such a blessing to spend time with loved ones and to share that time with our children.

The kids enjoyed the trips and looked forward to seeing their relatives each year. My husband Mac and I would take turns driving throughout the night.

I enjoyed driving through the desert late at night. The drive was serene and peaceful. It felt like we were the only people on the road during the late night drive. My husband would wake up and wonder where we were because I drove with the pedal to the floor in the quietness of the night.

The kids walked around and took sightseeing trips through each state that we stopped in. The trips were so memorable and lovely for the entire family.

Chapter 4 - Animal Lover

My mother and father raised us on a farm. We had all types of animals on the farm, and we were taught to care for them and love them just as if they were family. We respected each animal and were grateful for what they provided us. My parents raised cows, pigs, and chickens.

Every fall, my mother received a shipment of 50 baby chicks. The baby chicks came in from a farm in Memphis, Tennessee. The mailman delivered the chicks, and my mother grew so excited. She called them her "little biddies."

My father took great care of preparing their pen and chicken coop to ensure that they were protected and kept warm.

My father would put the sand down in the front of the coop. The coop was surrounded by chicken wire so they could spend time out in the sun during the day. My father placed a lantern in the sand to keep the chicks warm. At night the chicks stayed close to the sand and the lit lantern so they could remain warm and sleep.

My parents taught us how to appreciate and regard every animal on the farm. Every living creature had a purpose on this Earth. I passed this affection down to my children. I wanted them to understand the importance of every living thing that God placed on the Earth.

My mother's parents owned and operated a Bee Farm in Memphis. This is where my mother was raised, so she always had an affinity for animals and living creatures.

As far as I can remember, my family has been ardent caretakers of animals. That gene has passed on to my son as well. Billy was a lover of animals. He had two German Shepherds and an American Bulldog who were very intelligent.

He gave the German Shepherds biblical names because he was very active in the Youth Ministry. The female was Sheba, the male was Solomon, and the male bulldog was Domino.

Billy and Randy were active in Sunday School Ministry, Youth Department Ministry, and Church Ministries. The German Shepherds loved children; if one of the kids fell in the yard or any other place, the dogs would run over very quickly and comfort the child. The dogs would be the first ones to come to take care of the children.

The American Bulldog was a beautiful white dog with red eyes. He could talk. If we asked him a question when we came home from some place, he would start stretching, looking, and making talking sounds. He would be very happy to see us. During a hot summer day, Billy took him for a walk. I believe it was too long of a walk for Domino, especially in the heat.

Billy was devastated when Domino collapsed during their walk.

Mr. Wallace, a friend of the family, came by in his truck and helped Billy get Domino on the truck to get him home after he collapsed. After we got him home, we called the animal doctor immediately. The doctor said the cause of death was due to heart failure.

Those dogs were loving and caring, and both of them died of old age. Billy buried his dog in the woods. I know how much it hurt him to bury the dog because he didn't request another pet after losing Sheba and Solomon. He was so heartbroken at the loss of his precious pets.

Chapter 5 – The Trouble With Tuck

Billy was a student in Middle School when his teacher assigned a book for the class to review. Many students disliked doing book reviews because of the time and dedication that it took, but not Billy. An avid reader by his own right, he didn't mind reading the book and writing about his thoughts concerning the story.

He read the book with enthusiasm. I could immediately tell that he was reading something that piqued his interest. When he did something that interested him, Billy was almost unstoppable.

Billy's book review, *The Trouble with Tuck* by Theodore Taylor, Doubleday received acclaim and praise. I think that there was more of a personal appeal about the book that held his interest.

This book was about a young girl who adored her golden Labrador. The dog was her best friend from the moment he was placed in her grasp. Helen, the young girl, loved and cared for her puppy. The story tells the life of her dog from its youth onward.

I believe that Billy liked the book so much because of his affinity for dogs. He thought about Sheba and Solomon when he read the book. We talked about *The Trouble with Tuck* while Billy was reading it, and I listened intently as my son shared his feelings and thoughts.

His ability to comprehend was impressive. The way he saw things was also a beautiful sight to witness. Billy's mind worked in such an interesting fashion that it sometimes left me mesmerized.

Billy was always a thoughtful child and his wisdom shined through his writing. When he submitted the book review to his teacher, she was also astounded. She submitted his paper to an academic review board, who suggested that it be published.

This review was in the Book Award –Detroit Free Press. It will soon be a prime-time T.V. special. It is about a dog going blind and the obstacles the young owner went through with her pet.

The girl went to a school of companion dogs for the blind to get a leader dog for her dog. This book is very interesting and different from other books he has read. He really liked it. He was 11 years old and in the 6th grade when he wrote this book review.

"The goal of parenting isn't to create perfect kids. It's to point our kids to the perfect God" – Lindsey Bell.

Chapter 6 - Youth Director and Sunday School Teacher

Church played a pivotal role in our lives growing up. In fact, my grandfather was a preacher. I saw my grandfather preach on occasion. It was a fascinating sight. I was captivated by it all the sermons, the music, and the church itself. I sang in the church choir for years. Everything made me feel safe and contented. We used to walk to his church on Sundays. I recall the mourner's bench as a child.

The mourner's bench was instituted by the founder of the Methodist Church, John Wesley. Saints and sinners alike would sit at the bench to confess their sins and receive sanctification. It didn't take me long to decide to get baptized.

I also taught Sunday school from the age of 10 until I was about 14 years old. Teaching was always in my blood. Combining both teaching and the gospel was an astounding thing.

I enjoyed everything about the church. During this time, I also found myself teaching my youngest brother to read. He had some difficulty with reading comprehension. I recalled how one of my teachers would whoop the students who struggled with reading, so I tried the tactic with my brother.

My mother saw me disciplining my brother and quickly stopped me. She told me that I should try a different approach, one that involved encouragement instead. That changed everything for me. I taught my brother and, eventually, my students with encouragement as opposed to punishment.

My parents kept us involved in the church and education. We never missed a Sunday service, and it was something that my entire family loved doing together.

Since we had such a strong Methodist background, my husband and I decided to raise our children in the church as well. I wanted my children to experience the same relationship with the church where we attended.

Christian education was just as important as public school education. We were dedicated and enjoyed serving others for the Lord. This involved teaching different children from all types of family backgrounds and bringing them all together to teach them the Word of the Lord.

We joined Bethel Baptist Church in Albion, Michigan, when our children were young. Billy was only 15 months when we started attending the church. Over 30 years later, we still have strong ties to the church.

We forged many relationships at our church that are still strong to this day. One of the most memorable people at the church was Ms. Dee. Ms. Dee worked with our children from a very young age. She had such a calming spirit, and the children really took to her. They grew to love and respect her.

We were also Sunday school teachers. Ms. Dee was a faithful and dedicated member of our church.

She was also a mentor of sorts. I met her when I was in my early 30s. I was pregnant with my daughter Sandy when we began working for the church. I admired the fact that Ms. Dee didn't speak ill of anyone. She maintained such a pure and sweet disposition that everyone within the congregation wanted to be near her. I think about what she taught me to this day and smile at the memories that we made.

My children adored her and thought quite highly of her teachings. As a 60-year-old woman, she seemed more like a grandparent to them, but to me, she shared wisdom and knowledge that were unmatched. Her youngest daughter was the same age as Randy. The children all learned about the Word of God together under her teachings, and it was one of the greatest adventures ever.

Her love for the children was so passionate. We were very thankful and grateful that she was in our lives, and she played a major role in many of the fun activities organized at the church. As a young woman, she never shooed me away, and Ms. Dee consulted with me before making any decisions about the Sunday School teachings. It was refreshing and an experience that I will always cherish.

We buried Ms. Dee, our Youth Leader, and Sunday School Teacher, the day after Memorial Day. I was her Youth Director and assistant for several years, so I was deeply saddened to hear about her death at the age of eighty-three years old.

I believe that God places people in our lives for a reason. Ms. Dee was placed within my family's path to help enrich our lives and to add both wisdom and understanding. She will truly be missed.

Chapter 7 - Church Ministries

Pastor Earl was our church's minister. His wife played the piano, and his son was one of Billy's friends. They did everything together, whether it was in the church or at school. We had field trips with the church going to many different places such as apple orchards, pumpkin patches, cider mills, amusement parks, and basketball games. We even had a church basketball team.

Our children had many ways to remain involved, and we were sure to keep them engaged in all of the activities.

We picked apples at the orchard, and we used the apples to make applesauce. In the fall, we visited the pumpkin patch and everyone chose a pumpkin. After we returned from the pumpkin patch, they carved the pumpkins. We had pumpkin carving contests, and the best looking three pumpkins got prizes. The same pumpkins were used to decorate the Halloween Party at the church. We had the Spook House, Apple Bobbing, Pin the Tail on Donkey, Musical Chairs, Chili Dogs, Popcorn, Cupcakes, and other Goodies.

Most years, we went to Cedar Point Amusement Park in Ohio. My husband drove the bus. The children thoroughly enjoyed themselves every time we took the trip. Even though the ride was long, we still had fun!

We left early in the morning and returned late on a Saturday night. Cedar Point had many exciting rides; they were a blast!

The Youth Department hosted major plays during Easter and Christmas celebrations. The play at Easter time would be about Jesus being crucified, and He died on the cross for our sins. The first play was called, "He

Was The King of The Jews." The second play was called,
"He Came To Save the World From Our Sins."

Billy was a Junior Deacon along with other young boys.
They did devotion every second Sunday of each month.
They sang songs, read scriptures, and prayed for the
opening of church services. It was good training for the
young boys. The Senior Deacons were their mentors.
We had excellent teaching at our church.

Pastor Earl passed away at a very young age. We were
so sad! Billy was very young, too. Things have not been
the same since we lost him as our pastor. So, Billy
hasn't been active as a young man at church. Billy went
away to a private high school in Indiana, and he stayed
away for a great deal of the time due to the passing of
Pastor Earl.

Chapter 8 – High School Challenge

Billy started high school in the community, but we soon realized that there was a problem. My once enthusiastic student was now disenfranchised with his education. Billy began to grow bored with school. He didn't come home with the same excitement in his eyes as he did previously. I could tell that there was a significant change.

The classes were not challenging enough for him so, he asked if we could find a new high school. I had several conferences with his high school counselor, Ms. Avis, who understood what Billy was experiencing at school. As an educator, Ms. Avis was a colleague of mine, so she decided to level with me. "Your son isn't going to be challenged within the public school system," she confessed. After years of witnessing Billy's academic prowess, I knew that she was 100% correct.

Once my husband and I realized this, we decided to seek private education for Billy. Ms. Avis was instrumental in locating the perfect school for our gifted son.

She helped us search for a private school that would meet his academic and social development as a whole person. She was one of the counselors in the school community.

Chapter 9 - Military School

After an extensive investigation of high schools, we agreed that a prestigious military school was the best fit for Billy. The tuition was over $10,000 per year, and it was totally worth the cost. Billy was excited to begin his new life at the school.

The fall of the next school year, Billy began his new educational experience away from home . He was very young. The students lived in the dormitory. Most of his friends were from Chicago, so he had to make adjustments to his new lifestyle.

My husband and I were quite proud of Billy and the way he immediately took to his education journey. Billy was always self-driven, so he made decisions and followed through with them without anyone's help.

He did get homesick. One Saturday evening, he decided that he was going to walk home, which was approximately 100 miles away. He left campus without anyone knowing. After a while, he was missed. Later that same afternoon, we got a call that they could not find him. They were frightened and didn't know what to do. We were also frightened.

Billy's journey was a dark and cold night on a country road. The only things he heard were night noises and barking dogs. He saw headlights from cars far away. His thoughts were to go back to campus to be safe.

The Headmaster made his last call to me and his daddy around 8:00 P.M. Everyone had a peaceful night. All had gone well. He promised everyone that he would never attempt to do such a scary thing again.

The students wore uniforms. The daily uniforms were blue with a stripe and black patent shoes with a hat. The dress uniforms were white and with a hat and black patent shoes. The students were brought home on the school bus for the holidays. Students attended school there from several states in the United States.

When Billy was a senior, he was a starter on the basketball team. His basketball skills were very advanced. He played the forward position. The team traveled around Indiana playing ball. The school had the best season in 22 years that year. The boys made history for the school.

The senior trip was to London, Paris, and Madrid. That was a lifetime experience for all the students. In Paris, the locals drank wine, which they referred to as organics. During the trip, Billy saw youngsters in the country drinking organic drinks, so he decided to sneak from the group and get him a glass of it. He had drunk about a fourth of the glass by the time the Masters found him. His scapegoat was, he was thirsty, and the other youngsters were drinking it, too. From then on, he had to be watched closely.

Billy's inquisitive and impulsive mind often resulted in misunderstandings. If he saw something that intrigued him, he was drawn to it like a moth to a flame. It didn't matter that he could possibly get in trouble; all he cared about was the experience or satisfying his interests. While others may be deterred by the possibility of trouble, Billy gravitated towards anything that he took an interest in. This self-guided truth-seeking followed Billy from his youth well into adulthood.

At a school as prestigious as this, the headmasters had difficulty with self-directed children. It didn't help that Billy suffered from stomach troubles, which forced him away from the group. His problem was using the restroom many times. He felt bad about his situation.

The Head Master called us the minute they returned home to the States. We were very disappointed in his behavior.

He was punished by not going on our family's last vacation for the summer. He spent that week with his grandmother and grandfather. The sidewinder did not complain at all. He just took it like a grown man. Billy was highly educated. He felt lonely at times, but he stayed and graduated with honors.

TO ALL HEADMASTERS, THANK YOU FOR A JOB WELL DONE!

Chapter 10 – Randy

Randy was a talented wrestler. He was thin, but he had the ability to pin his opponents to the mat effortlessly. He won several letters for wrestling in high school. I enjoyed watching my son wrestle. I was my son's loudest cheerleader! I would cheer him on from the stands. The team grew used to hearing me yell, "Randy! Don't let them get you down!"

He could hear me shouting my encouragement, and I believe it helped boost his morale during the matches.

The team often remarked about how I encouraged them to play harder.

Randy was always a gifted reader. When our children were young, we introduced them to the enjoyment that books brought. He never deviated from reading. Like Billy, Randy could be found in his room sitting on the bed, fully immersed within a book.

As a result, Randy graduated from the high school in the community with honors. He received several awards in academics and most of the sports. He also earned a 4-Year Scholarship to an esteemed HBCU. He majored in Business Administration with a minor in Finance and earned a job with the United States Army.

Randy was sworn into the Army in January 1990 as a candidate for the United States Military Academy Preparatory School ten months before enrolling in the Army ROTC Program at the HBCU.

He received his commission as a Finance Officer in the Army Reserves in August 1995.

He transitioned over to acquiring and managing residential apartment buildings from 1998 thru present in Washington D.C. and Detroit. Now Randy serves as; Lieutenant Colonel United States Army Reserves.

Randy is married to Jocelyn, and they have two children, Elizabeth and William.

Chapter 11 - Sandy

Sandy is Billy's only sister. He is eight years older than her. She is a gifted tennis player who has played the sport since she was seven years old. A good friend of mine was an avid tennis player, and she took Sandy out to the tennis court to teach her. It was wonderful watching my young daughter skillfully hit the ball.

Sandy loved to play tennis and earned a four-year varsity letter. She was also an excellent basketball player. She played basketball throughout elementary and middle school. I coached her 7th-grade basketball team and loved every minute.

Not only was she athletically talented, but she was also academically gifted. Sandy was inducted into the National Honor Society in high school and eventually became president. She was an outstanding student and graduated with high honors and great leadership ability from the high school in the community.

She received several scholarships, awards, and recognitions. Sandy also earned a 4-Year Academic Scholarship to a State University in Michigan, where she continued to excel in tennis.

She graduated with a degree in Elementary Education with a Minor in English. Sandy graduated from college with high honors. She did a one-year internship in Northfield's Public Schools.

Her teaching career started the very next school year in the public school system. During her first year of teaching, she completed her Masters in Curriculum and Teaching. She taught within the public school system for ten years.

She and her husband have two young sons,. Her husband is an anointed minister and also Lieutenant Commander in the United States Navy.

She is involved with her children's early education. I'm proud of the woman and mother that my daughter has become.

She is a loving wife and mother who is God-fearing and treats everyone with the utmost respect. She enjoys activities, such as traveling, spending time with family, sharing her personal testimony, and being a living witness to those she encounters on a daily basis.

She is concerned with being a positive role model for the youth and living a life that is pleasing to God. Sandy is also a member of Alpha Kappa Alpha Sorority. She believes in serving all mankind. She wants the world to be a better place to live in.

Chapter 12 – The University Experience

After graduation and spending a hot summer in Georgia, Billy entered the University as a freshman. He lived in the dormitory. Dormitory living brought back high school memories. Although this University was much bigger than the military academy, Billy still had to make adjustments.

The University is located in Washington, D.C., which is a world away from Michigan, as it seemed. He attended one of the top Historically Black Colleges and Universities in the nation. We were proud of our son for not only being accepted at this University but for also receiving a full scholarship.

As a part of his first introduction to the university community, the staff planned an extensive New Student

Orientation Program. An integral part of this program was called "Campus Pals," that personally helped Billy to adjust to the University. He was very active with the group. They worked with school-aged children, doing many activities in the community.

Although attending college was a wonderful experience for Billy, he also experienced bouts of homesickness. He wanted to spend some time in Michigan.

Randy attended a military preparatory school in New York and then transferred the following year to the same university where his brother attended. This helped them both with the homesickness. Once Billy entered his sophomore year of college, we purchased them a condo on 14th street in Washington, DC. We also bought them bicycles, which they rode around town and back and forth to school.

Randy still has his bicycle. He maintained all of his belongings quite well and took great care of everything that we gave him. In fact, Randy still has his Hot Wheel car collection and a train set that my husband and I gave him one year for Christmas. I have always been proud and in awe of the way he cared for things.

We purchased a car for the boys when they were nearing their senior year of college. They drove home to Michigan from D.C. a few times per year, and it was so exciting. They would honk the horn as they pulled into the driveway. You couldn't tell me that the president himself wasn't visiting the way we carried on. My husband, Sandy, and I would run out to meet them.

Our family was quite close, and it was a beautiful sight to see.

Matthew 5:4

Blessed are those who mourn, for they will be comforted.

Chapter 13 – Family Tragedy

My husband and I raised our children with love and care. We always envisioned growing old together. God's plans are much different than ours at times. Our thoughts and plans can be altered in the blink of an eye. One evening while my beloved husband was traveling home from work in Chicago on I-94, he had a fatal car accident.

When I received the news about my husband's death, I was absolutely devastated. My daughter was in college at Michigan State. She and her friends were heading on a trip to Chicago when we received the terrible news. I told her friends not to let her come home because I knew that she needed to do something to distract her from the tragic loss. Sandy was inconsolable when she heard the news.

Billy was in Michigan visiting at the time. I told him the news, and he completely lost it. He hollered until his voice was hoarse. Billy was so close to his father that the loss was completely debilitating for him. It was equally as devastating for Randy as well. My children loved their father. I felt awful for my children, and I also felt the loss of my best friend. Mac was only 55 years old when he died.

The accident was so tragic that it was reported all over the national news. Mac was such a kind and loving person that his death drew people from far and wide. My home was filled with mourners who wanted to offer their condolences.

Women from the church came to my home and cooked meals for us. People from the community brought us meals as well. They also cleaned the house from top to bottom and tried to help me in any way that they could.

I was very appreciative. The driveway was lined with large trucks from drivers who knew my husband. Some people didn't know Mac personally, but they were affected by the tragedy.

I had so many people inside my home during the week of my husband's funeral; I had to stay with one of my friends because there was no space at my home. It was lovely to see how many people cared about my husband.

My husband's mother passed away when he was very young. His eldest sister Katie loved him so much. She sent for him to live with her in Los Angeles when he was just a young boy, and she continued to raise him. Katie and her children came to our home in Michigan to celebrate Mac's life.

It was their first time visiting our home in Michigan. I know that my husband would have been so proud for his sister to see the life he created for himself and his family.

I felt so supported with everyone there to comfort me.

I could tell that my husband's death was traumatic for my children, but it was especially hard for Billy. I don't believe that he has ever recovered.

It rained for over 20 minutes the day of my husband's funeral; then suddenly, the sun came out. I felt like my husband was letting me know that he was right by my side during this difficult time. My children and I still mourn the significant loss of my husband, Mac. I am truly blessed to have had him in my life for as long as I did, although I wish it had been longer.

The Sidewinder

A person who lives according to his or her own wishes and beliefs, unconstrained by society's conventions.

Chapter 14 – Free Spirit

After college graduation, Billy was hired to work for the District of Columbia. He was not ready for the workplace. He played around and did a lot of silly things at work and was very immature. He was not responsible, so he was let go from his position.

He came home to Michigan got a good job in his field, which was in Information Systems at an Outstanding Cooperation in Southfield. He was highly recommended by one of my mother's students. He played the same tricks. I guess he just wasn't cut out to work.

I know that he is intelligent and capable of doing great things, but sometimes I struggle with the fact that he doesn't use all of his potential. I see all of his intelligence and intellect going to waste at times. Billy has the ability to do many great things. I long for the day in which he recognizes and uses that ability.

Sometimes, I just think he is lazy. Then other times, I am reminded of how he changed once his father passed away. I wonder if he lost the will to succeed and grow once we tragically lost Mac. I know that it was a life-changing situation, but I wish that he understood how many things he could achieve if he let go of whatever insecurity or fear that is holding him back.

I often talked to Billy about him getting a job and filling out the applications, but when they call, he just does not respond! He was always using an excuse. The corporate world isn't for Billy. He is searching for something that will pique his interests and intrigue. I fear that those things cannot be found in a regular 9-5 job.

The pandemic is not making things much easier. We are all feeling the effects of the quarantine. The job hunt scene is shrinking, and so are my hopes that he will find something that he enjoys doing.

As much as I love my son, I had to take a step back from supporting him financially. Things are getting tight now. I stopped giving him any more money or answering his telephone calls. I know that he needs a job, even though he gets food stamps and insurance from the state.

I'm getting old now. So, I'm not able to take care of Billy anymore. I'm now seventy-five years old. He needs to take responsibility for his life. I have provided him with a little car and a place to live. Billy told me that he is thinking positively about getting himself a job. He has been living on his own for nine months now.

This is a new year, and he decided he was going to get a job in his field, Information Systems. He would like to take care of his daughter, Amya, instead of her mother, brother, and sister, taking care of her. Amya is Billy's pride and joy. She currently lives in Jackson, Michigan, with her lovely mother. Billy gets so excited when Amya achieves something or does well in school. Mia is

Amya's mother. She is a beautiful person on the inside and out. She loved my son with a steadfastness that can be admired. I truly believe that she is the love of his life. Mia is a terrific mother who supports both Amya and Billy at times. She is brilliant and has stuck by my son's side. Every year we take the children on a holiday trip. One year we were heading to Battle Creek for Randy's ceremony, and Billy was late to the event.

I admonished him for his tardiness. My granddaughter, Amya, was only three years old at the time, but she quickly said something to me. She said, "oh, mother, please don't fuss at my daddy like that." We were so tickled by how quickly she stood up for her father that we both fell out laughing.

Amya is a bright girl and was articulate at such a young age, just like her father. I am proud of the way my son loves his child and the love she has for her father.

I think that once he obtains a job in his field, things will be better for Billy. All it takes is that one blessing to lead to a life-changing breakthrough. As a woman of faith, I believe that God will bless Billy with the perfect job that will help boost his self-esteem and finances. As long as he continues to try and put forth the effort, he will be blessed one day with a beautiful result.

I share this because I know that Billy's story will be an inspiration for others.

Billy would often say, "I am seriously looking for a job! I will get a good job very soon. I'm thanking God." And that's Billy the Sidewinder.

Dorothy Brown Perkins has done journaling all of her life. Her writings have been selected to be placed on bulletin boards in classrooms, in contests, and in newspapers. She hears God's voice as she sits still and focuses on Him. Jesus' voice comes as spontaneous thoughts. She journals the flows and pictures from Him.

She grew up in Cotton Plant, Arkansas. She graduated from high school with top honors. She received a Bachelors Education from the University of Arkansas and Theological Curriculum and a Masters in Education from Eastern Michigan University and Western Michigan University with honors.

Dorothy is a retired teacher from Michigan Public Schools and resides in Albion, Michigan.

www.ingramcontent.com/pod-product-compliance
Lightning Source LLC
Chambersburg PA
CBHW060419050426
42449CB00009B/2036